FRAMING MEMORIES

First Printing 2011

ISBN 978-0-9815560-6-2

Harbor Mountain Press, Inc., is a 501(c)(3) organization dedicated
to works of high literary merit. Harbor Mountain Press books are
distributed by Small Press Distribution, a non-profit organization,
through GenPop Books and Distribution, and through our website.
The Press appreciates your support.

SERIES EDITOR
Peter Money

DESIGN
Heron Graphic Arts

COVER ART
Detail from "Incommunicado" by Bob Stang

Harbor Mountain Press
PO Box 519
Brownsville, VT 05037

harbormountainpress.org

FRAMING MEMORIES

MARIO SUSKO

Harbor Mountain Press
Vermont

ACKNOWLEDGMENTS

A selection of these poems appeared in a chapbook *Rules of Engagement* published in 2009 by erbacce-press, Liverpool (UK). "The Bridge," "Where We Go," Sooner or Later," "The Order of Things," and "The Color of Blood" appeared in Vol. 31 of the cyber anthology *the other voices international project* (2007). "Where We Go" was published in the 2008 and "The Conduct of War" in the 2009 anthology of the CCNY Annual Spring Poetry Festival *Poetry in Performance*; "Relations" and "Execution" appeared in *Stranger at Home*, an anthology edited by A. Gritsman et al. (New York: Numina Press, 2008).

The following poems have appeared in print and electronic journals, sometimes in a slightly different form: "The Aftermath," "At the Window," "The Bridge," "Cine Film," "The Color of Blood," "Compatriots and Enemies," "Congruities," "Dead Language," "End Phrase," "Execution," "First Day of Spring," "Fools of Fate," "Framed Memories," "Growing up with Sin," "Homeward Bound," "In the Classroom," "In the Supermarket Half a World Away," "Mise en scene," "A Note. A Dot.," "Of Belonging," "Of Breathing and Living," "Of Roosters, Sex, and Semblances," "Of Time, Memory, and the Soul," "On the Way out," "The Order of Things," "The Other Side," "A Poet on the Sidewalk," "The Question of the Beginning and the End," "The Question of Sides," "Relations," "Rules of Engagement," "Slides," "Sooner or Later," "The Sum of Everything," "Telling Stories," "There and Here," Tradeable Commodities," "Traversing," "Walking away," "The Way Things Happen," "What I Want to Say," and "Where We Go." Grateful acknowledgment is made to the editors of the following journals: *Andwerve, Argestes Literary Review, Ars Interpres* (Sweden), *Borderlands: Texas Poetry Review, Broken Bridge Review, Default* (Ireland), *Dream Catcher* (UK), *Earthshine, erbacce* (UK), *Iconoclast, LanguageandCulture.net, Long Island Sounds 2008, Long Island Sounds 2009, Main Channel Voices, The Main Street Rag, Meridian Anthology of Contemporary Poetry, Minnetonka Review, Nassau Review, Oracle, Orbis* (UK), *Parameter Magazine* (UK), *Pilvax Magazine* (Hungary), *The Progressive, Red Wheelbarrow, Relief: A Quarterly Christian Expression, Sentinel Literary Quarterly* (UK), *Taj Mahal* (India), and *Tule Review.*
"Execution" was nominated by *Dream Catcher* (UK) for the 2007 and "In the Classroom" for the 2009 Forward Poetry Prize in the best single poem category. *Argestes Literary Review* nominated "Relations" for the 2009 Pushcart Prize; "There and Here" was given the Editor's Choice Award in Poetry by *Relief: A Quarterly Christian Expression* (2008, Vol. 2, No. 1)
Thanks to Nassau Community College for a sabbatical that provided time to complete the manuscript. Thanks to Robert Karmon and Bruce Urquhart for their reading and suggestions; also, special thanks to Peter Money, the editor, for his unwavering support and guidance.

CONTENTS

One:

Two:

So that's life, then: things as they are?
W. Stevens

Per racontare tutta la storia dovresti
tornare dai morti.
E. Noferi

One: Rules
     of
     Engagement

RETRACING THE STORY

there may come a day, a good day,
to retrace the story and see whether I
was still there when and if it ended,
part of what happened along the way
and made things turn out as they did.

I'll go out, walk to the same corner
that was in the passage I remember I
was in, though perhaps in some other
story, and managed to get out on instinct,
the day that looked deceptively descriptive,

nothing to indicate that that could change
the course of the plot, the history, or
end right there because it had not rained
the day before and the blood on the sidewalk
meant that the message had found its target,

received before having been perceived,
the foreshadowing of reality misleading,
life saved to be lost, or life lost to be
saved, like looking to the right, or looking
to the left, the ending without resolution,

as the day I came to the corner, again,
lingered there, waiting for the blood
under the new layer of cement on the sidewalk,
my blood, to tell me whether life stopped there
and the story went on, or the other way round.

WHERE WE GO

how far back would you have to go
to get beyond the beginning of nothingness
and how long would it take you to return
with a clump of dirt and a fistful of seeds
to plant them and have life grow again –

I sit at your bed while you sleep,
tell you stories that come from nowhere
and do not go anywhere, though they help
me not to lose my sanity when there is
no one around to keep me awake come evening.

I cannot see where you might have gone
tonight, and tomorrow I'll be reluctant
to ask, knowing I don't like to be reminded
of the graves that need to be visited,
when I just stare at mounds, wordless.

Your fingers twitch as if trying to point
in a certain direction, and I touch the tip
of your index finger with mine, impeding
its upward movement, afraid your whole being
will rise, leaving me to face the empty space.

Two heavy comforters shroud your breath,
which makes me put a mirror to your face
to be sure you're still here, and when I look
at the cracked glass your image smiles at me,
though your hands are now made into a fist.

GROWING UP WITH SIN

Don't stick your tongue out; it's a sin,
mother would admonish me whenever I
looked at my rich neighbor's kid bite
smugly into a paralyzing aroma of his
ham and cheese sandwich, the two slices
of bread white like snow, so different
from my mud looking, paprika and lard
covered slab that smelled of manure.

for mother everything we didn't have, or
she had no confident answer to was a sin:
why my father got her pregnant while she
was in high school, thus making me a product
of sin, one frail moment, as she'd later put
it, we have to atone for as long as we live.

whenever I thought of my friend's sister,
my mind picturing her in the kitchen
cupboard, behind the misted glass, wrapped
in a towel though naked underneath,
dropping it painfully slowly, my pupils
became narrow slits, those of a cat, fixed,
unlike camera lens in American movies,
on her budding cherry nipples, mother
would read me and say, **You are not
having one of those sinful thoughts, are you,**
and I would blink, pretending I didn't get
what she meant, and ask for a glass
of milk, for her the only sign of purity,
for me nothing more than a lumpy mix
of water and chalk-tasting powder.

I itch, I blurted out one evening
when she walked into the room and yelled,
You're not touching yourself, are you,
though by that time I had rewound repeatedly
the day my father's tipsy sister lifted
her skirt to show me what women had and I

stared stunned at something that looked
like my uncle's mouthless goatee.

once a month mother would push
me into a lacquered dark oak booth
and I gazed through a lattice partition
that resembled the top of a Linzer torte,
trying to recognize a ruddy impassive face
as I invented my ridiculous little sins:
chased the neighbor's chickens in the yard,
broke off a lilac branch in the park,
tried, at one time, my aunt's silk bloomers
to feel their softness, the latter provoking
a slight chuckle behind the screen, followed
by a feigned cough and a stern command to say
three Hail Marys before I go to sleep that night.

You'll never be able to forget, she told me
half a century later and half a world away,
dying in a city of her exile, **if you do not
forgive those who sinned against you, when they
tried to kill you, and that is also sinful,**
only to have me realize as I barked into
the clammy receiver, **With all that sin business
of yours, oh, my God, you have created a misfit,
a mental cripple just like yourself,** that I
had, at the end, become her awaited executioner.

OF ROOSTERS, SEX, AND SEMBLANCES

One late foggy afternoon, he says, as I
stand at his bed, holding a spoon and a plate
with a beguiling cure-all chicken soup, pieces
of meat with bones, the stomach, the heart,
the liver there, everything I've thrown in,
hoping that would help him regain his strength,
Mother came home carrying a rooster
Under her coat, a skinny bird with mean eyes
Though a glorious black and red plumage.

No one in the neighborhood had one
In those days after the war, nor did we
Have money to afford such a creature.
She kept him in the kitchen, a prisoner
Of war almost, and I concluded she had
Stolen him during one of her excursions,
As she called them, into the scattered hamlets
Across the river, in search of some real food.

The rooster grew stronger and bigger,
So she clipped his wings to prevent him
From jumping onto the coal chest and chairs,
Though his ludicrous hopping around
Made me angry, as did my mother's remark
Each time he spread his useless wings,
Extended his neck and crowed: The sun
Is not rising, but I know what is.

I ate that rooster, feathers and all,
Many times in my dreams, though mother
Kept saying: Never a good soup does a rooster
Make, but some eggs by you would be a help.

I dared not ask her what that would change
Until one day a rich neighbor's daughter,
A red-haired nymph I dreamed of conquering
After I dealt with a dragon in the thicket,
Smuggled her father's book and showed me

A drawing of a man in pointed slippers
Atop a woman with a red mark on her forehead
And anthracitous hair that cascaded
Down her naked breasts: That's what roosters
Do to hens to make eggs, she declared.

She took me down into the basement, he
whispers haltingly, staring at the ceiling
as if retrieving the memory from the shapes
the flames of three candles play with,
Sprawled on two potato sacks in her cubicle,
Pulling me down like a rag doll on top of her.
I felt dull pain in my knees and prickling
In my groin as if an army of ants had
Suddenly invaded my shorts; her lavender hair
Made me dizzy and I was relieved when a moment
Later she laughed witchlike and pushed me
Off her: See, she said, nothing to it, her eyes
Aglow like the rooster's in our kitchen.

That night, while shivering in my bed, my eyes
Shut tight as I was trying to banish the drawing
And the girl's rose-pimpled legs from my mind,
I kept repeating to myself: O God, merciful God,
Please don't have her lay an egg tomorrow.

CINE FILM

as a child I would often wake up at night
- father's unhinged hand slapping my mother's
cheek, her rasping cry traveling like echo
from the kitchen, a freight train rattling
the windows, a neighbor upstairs slamming
down a toilet seat, or utter silence suddenly
screaming in my head – and try to close
my eyes as quickly as I could, as if dropping
out of the dream was nothing else
but some unwanted, yet repairable malfunction

something the reel man, as we children used
to call him, had to deal with when the cine
film snapped and the spool started to clank
in the drum, only to have the images burst
onto the screen again almost instantaneously,
the violins regain their pitch and two mouths
continue their slow drawing closer together
like two train carriages about to be coupled.

I admired the old reel man's dexterity,
a quick snip with the scissors, or a blade,
a touch of glue, I surmised, and the world
would be moving again, the whistles
and shouts in the pit die down, sometimes
followed by discordant clapping. I would
always turn my head to see him peer
through the hole, his eyes aglow in the light
of the shimmering arc, his content look
a message the interruption was negligible.

booing and shouting, mine too, would
never be followed by applause if something
like that happened during a documentary
preshow, as it did that fated summer night
while we watched a camera pen soundlessly
across the faces of ghosts behind barbed
wire, then zoom on naked bodies scooped up

by a bulldozer, suddenly freeze, jerk, and go
dead, as if it got ripped off, leaving the screen
tremble in the grip of the unnatural beam,
causing an eruption of shouts and feet stomping.

we were quickly ushered out with a promise
our ticket would be honored the following night,
and as I pushed my way through cigarette clouds
and jostling bodies on the sidewalk I saw
our reel man, his mouth open, eyes glazed,
carried out on a stretcher, his forearm hanging
off the side, a tattooed number like animal's
teeth marks stamping itself on my mind.

for a long time after that I wasn't able to fall
asleep, my eyes glued to the spectral light
and the window bars the street lamp kept leaving
on the ceiling, and though every night I recalled
my mother's words to count slowly as long as I
could to have my mind drift away the only numbers
that would come to me were seven one two one zero.

CONGRUITIES

warm november rain, glazed trees
still not having cut the blood to all
the leaves, letting them hope the nature
of the given can be fooled by the phenomenal:

- I am not that old yet to die – she said,
looking at the pale red line across her chest,
clumps of hair stuck in the comb, lifeless
autumnal grass in the rake, and I mumbled,
- You'll get through this all right, you'll see –

it is again fear driven memory that draws
me to the window and the zooming drone
of a helicopter, its search light beam
that swoops up suddenly, snatching my mind away:

- Why me – she asked one day in the sunny kitchen,
staring at the white sparkling plate
with two pieces of chicken breasts, each with a speck
ready to begin its cellulous conquest,
- Can you answer that – while I was trying
to avoid my featureless reflection in the face
of her mute black wall clock, unlit cigarette
hanging from my lip an excuse to sneak out:

now its glow, like a firefly's mating call,
breathes rhythmically in the tinted window
of a car parked across, and I dare not let go
of the shade cord, as if my utter stillness
would make the growth disappear, and the answer
to unanswerable questions render them redundant:

- Take me home, I want you, now / Take me
home, I want you to, now – would it have been
easier for me to have pretended I'd heard
the former or the latter, as I stood, my back
turned to that bloodless room, gazing out
of the window at the blossom bedecked trees,

my fingers numb from gripping the pull-down cord,
my breath straining in vain not to fog the glass

REVISITING ONESELF

Is that what brings me again to this
grave, its letters chiseled in stone,
the first name that of my mother
whose resting place I know nothing about,
and has me sit on a small wooden bench
at its foot, trying to make myself believe
it was quite by chance I'd come upon it
and let my deadened memories impel my mind
to bring them back to life and deal with:

If your mother, she wrote, her handwriting
already death scribbling, wasn't capable
of loving you and your father never wanted
to love you because we both loved more
to hate each other it's quite understandable
that not being schooled in love you resorted
to that war of hatred within yourself but
that I think made you survive this war
so that some day somewhere we can revisit
ourselves and see whether we are whole enough
to be able to feel what love should truly be.

Unmoved summer day, lifeless, one might say,
not a breath of wind, mute, except for a bird
perched on an angel, singing its heart out:
why are birds always so joyous in a cemetery,
the thought I can't get rid of flutters aimlessly
in my head while I stare at the stone, waiting
for its pulsating letters to give me a hint.

Suddenly, the bird stops and flies off,
realizing, perhaps, its song was to no avail,
or telling me my time is up as well, so I
take off my shirt and lie onto the mound,
whispering into stiff blades that both caress
and prick my lips and the scar on my chest:

If you feel my heart now, it will tell you
two halved lives do not make one's life whole.

TRADEABLE COMMODITIES

does the eye know that it saw what it
was supposed to see and had the mind
print it, or does it receive beforehand
a mind generated picture and has it
superimposed upon the captured image –

once you're made to have no answer
to either, or an equally tenable answer
to both, you are told that you could not
have seen what you thought you'd seen:

because of the light, or the angle,
the configuration of the terrain, or
even more importantly, your own reading
into the actual event some kind
of pre-set perception of its causality,
which made you confuse the sight
with vision driven by memory reflection.

so, it shouldn't have come as a surprise
to you that, in the end, you were let go,
for anything you'd go back to later on
was to be brought into question, or
dismissed as nothing else but the sign
of a tendencious, even unstable, mind.

still, you kept on trying to have words
reflect what the eyes saw had happened,
though the more credible you wanted them
to appear, the more tradeable their meaning
turned out to be, and so did reality,
whether it was seen or thought of
as a brand-name or generic commodity.

DEAD LANGUAGE

I have to find a way
          out, he said, standing
behind the curtain,
if I am to remain sane

the eyes trace a course
the mind miscalculates the distance

          a blind bullet finds
a shortcut and strikes
          the latin teacher

someone laughs
at nothing   somewhere
          a reflex reaction
          a declension
of dead pronouns

don't go near
          the window
don't stay too long
          in one place

a bird crashes into the pane
a face meets its own face

Where would he go,
          I asked his wife,
Anywhere, anywhere   Away
even from himself

the body is taken down to the basement
all skin and bones weighing a ton
the name is crossed out
          on the tenants' food list

the bird with a broken wing
still   crouches on the ledge
as if waiting to be taken in
and saved or   made to fall off
        and end the misery

at night we leave the staircase
and descend,
        I to my cubicle
next to that where the body is
buried under an old mattress
with the towel over my face,
        forcing myself to dream
about sour cabbage, dijon mustard
and sausages,
        my mind running after the smell

        that's how I try
        to outpace insanity
though with every daybreak
my high school latin teacher's words
come back to me
        over and over again
nothing ever dies
unless   a man kills it.

THE CONDUCT OF WAR

from an old dank cardboard box in the cellar
I dumped out a whole forgotten battalion
of tin soldiers I used to play with as a kid.

how it got there and when I couldn't remember:
perhaps I outgrew wars or mother believed people
when they proclaimed: This war ended all wars.

it would have seemed so as I gazed silently
at my troops' once colorful uniforms, now
just faded patches, telling me they'd fought

in all decisive battles, their drawn swords
twisted or broken, many a base they stood on
gone, making them look as good as dead.

some without a hand or a leg I put carefully
back into the box, together with two wooden
horses, their head dangling on a shiny wire.

what I really needed now was a few tanks,
if nothing else some heavy artillery pieces,
for I knew the advanced armored units

had already reached the suburb, intent
on crossing the river behind my building
and linking up with the encamped mercenaries.

my army was the only thing that stood
in their way, yet no plan would I've been able
to devise that would save us from being overrun.

the following night, when the steady rumble
of tracks and engines began to drown out
the croaking of frogs at the river bank,

I painted with a crayon I found on the floor
a red cross sign on the box and put it
in the drum of a discarded washing machine.

I took those battle ready soldiers to the lobby
and set them down on the highest step, all
of us in a combat line facing the front door.

later, through half-closed eyes and the dark, I
saw a ten year old kid I grew up with burst in,
brandishing a wooden sword, a paper cocked hat

on his head, and we fought again, I, a twelve
year old veteran, swinging my mother's broomstick,
until we both fell exhausted and said: Truce.

RULES OF ENGAGEMENT

the road ended at a large wall,
a hole in it no doubt made by a tank,
a note scribbled above the hole read:
You need a key to go through –

I almost laughed and squeezed through
only to find myself face to face
with a solid wall and its note: You
must have a hole to go through a wall –

with my bare hands I dug a passage
underneath and on the other side,
having turned around, my eyes blinded
by a flashlight, I saw nothing –

Where am I, I cried out, where
is my home – and a megaphonic voice
answered: Wherever you think you are
going, you broke the rules of engagement,

so pick up that gun at your feet
and be ready to defend yourself.
At the end of the field there's a note
with instructions; read it carefully –

I went around, for I knew now
the field was dotted with mines,
and found a stopwatch hanging
from a branch, a piece of paper
pinned askew to the mossy trunk:

This is not a game, it said,
and for you to pass you need a wall
with a hole and key to go through,
then run straight across the field.
Leave the gun here – suddenly I realized
I held a starter's pistol – and go back.
You've got one minute to follow through.

ESCAPING BY CIRCLING

the word is that I am a proven survivor,
but how can I be that if I am still running
for my life, not even knowing
the only chance to escape I may be left with
will just make the radius a bit wider –

yet could that confuse those who want
to track me down, and if I, at some point
or by some miracle, manage to get
behind them, should I act as if I do not know
them and they, in turn, would not recognize me,

for that would, should I proceed ahead slowly,
give them enough reason to believe it's some
one else they ought to go after, not me really,
and if I continued to do that again and again
perhaps they would stop to figure out

whom they truly wanted to hunt down, but
that would force me to stop as well to try
and see what they ultimately came up with,
which could, no doubt, in lieu of someone
else, make me one more time a suitable target,

so I'd have to run, causing them to chase me,
mindless now of whether it's me or not, because
they are on a mission that must be accomplished,
and the only choice I'd have, if they finally catch
me, is to pretend they got someone else, not me

THE SNIPER AND I

Everyone having fled the building,
distraught by sniping and shelling, I moved
whatever food was left down into the cellar
and sat during the day in a cubicle, ignoring
the fact the mercenaries across the street
could raid the place any time they chose to.

I'd spend the night on a wooden board,
its bottomside resting on a discarded washing
machine, its topside on a chest without drawers,
the slightest motion to the right or the left
making me feel I was on a raft in heavy seas.

I slept like a dead man, my hands clasped
on my chest, my head supported by a tote
with a colorful advertisement sticker:
Visit Rome Feel at Home, or, conversely,
like a baby, if my mind suspended the senses.

I did not need an alarm clock to wake me up
in the morning, for at nine sharp a sniper
would begin his routine day at work, pecking
at the building like some giant woodpecker.

I began to rely on his german-like pedantry,
a ten minute respite between the rounds letting
me run up into the ground floor apartment
to relieve myself or collect drinking water.

Then one day there was silence and I overslept
for a good hour, quite angry when I woke up,
as if I had been let down, betrayed by a clock
whose batteries had suddenly gone dead.

I started to worry about the sniper, even myself:
what happened, was he up to some trick, came
into the vestibule to find a live target, or
was gone for not having done his job properly;
I almost wanted to venture out and yell: What is
going on here; I have the right to know.

The next day I sneaked up to one of the windows
upstairs, put a hat on the broomstick and had
it peak out, but nothing happened, not even when I
moved it to the left and to the right the way
a drunkard would, still battling a hang-over.

I waited two more days, going at dusk
through abandoned apartments, finding in one
a can of beans under the sofa; the second day,
as if to banish from my head imaginary sounds
from down below, I glanced out of the window
and saw three men sitting on a stoop
across the street, drinking beer, one of them
catching sight of me and pointing with his finger
in my direction before I managed to duck
and crawl away, my heart in my parched throat.

Flat on my raft that night, I stared numbly
at the corner, waiting for my last candle stump
to choke itself to death and wondering
why a spider would continue to spin its web
in a place where hopefulness was but a joke.

In the morning I heard steps in the vestibule
and went to see, making sure my hands were
in full sight, but a man I 'd never seen before
just glanced at me: It's over, he mumbled,
they signed the agreement two days ago;
anything of value in these apartments? I
scrambled out, blinded for a while by the sun,
and slowly managed to make out those three men
that again sat on the stoop, drinking beer.

Which one of you wanted to kill me, I shouted,
my voice both deranged and comical, and one
of them looked at me grinning and waved me
off, though I could descry through a gaping hole
in the front door frosted glass the barrels
of three sniper rifles leaning like fish poles
against the snow-white tiled wall.

ON THE WAY OUT

I tell you, at dawn I'm getting us
out of here, I said, sitting on a crate
that swayed on the ribbed cement floor,
its faded label, Jaffa Oranges, holding
onto one of the laths, making my mind
fool my stomach with a sudden whiff
of intoxicating aroma in the nostrils.

I just broke a slice of stale bread in half
and almost smiled, the act an ironic rendition
of afikoymen at seder I was part of
in my friend's plush Park Avenue apartment
on a quiet evening centuries ago,
his wife's mother's joking remark, uttered
like some refrain: when are we going to get
to wine, the only thing I was not ready for.

This is another world, and another life
I was not ready for; the front door dislodged
by mortar shells is held together by a rope,
hardly a mark to keep off the angels of death.

At daybreak, when the light begins to nibble
at the insides of darkness, we sneak out,
hugging the buildings' faces, walking in step
with the rhythm of distant explosions.
I count the doors, stop at the seventh entrance,
open, as I was informed it would be, and enter
the cave, feeling my every step; I point
at the ground floor apartment at the left,
abandoned, its door off the hinges letting me
see the balcony curtain dance in the breeze.
Once inside, as we meander, trying to avoid
dark shadowy edges of some overturned furniture,
I glance at the couch and there, placed
almost perfectly in the middle, a huge
saucer-eyed doll stares at me, its golden locks
and a long frilly dress, white as snow,

too visible to have been carried by those
who had fled, her arms stretched out
as though inviting us to join her for cookies,
figs and nuts, raisins and some sweet wine.

On the balcony, we go over the railing
and drop onto the parking lot, bend over,
zig-zagging among burned-out, mangled cars
till we reach the brook and slide down
the wet dirt; I take off my shoes, you, too,
the cold satiny water curling around
my ankles like bed-sheets in winter causing
the body to cringe like a caterpillar's
whenever, as a kid, I'd prick it with a stick,
driven by some inexplicable impulse to test
its pain tolerance, the act later taken only
as simple mischief, the gurgling sound of water
that of a lullaby making the mind drift
downstream all the way to some warm sea.

On the embankment, facing the open space,
a soccer field, goal-posts gone, we start
to run, and I feel your hand touch my back,
withdraw, touch again, as if to make sure
that I'm still there, or urge me to move faster.
Suddenly I sense something in my pants' pocket
presses against my thigh, hampering my stride,
yet beating in unison with my heart, and
then I realize you put it there to guide
us safely, that small cross your father made
of two pieces of wood tied with a soiled rope;
he kept it hidden in the concentration camp,
the only possession he managed to bring back,
and my eyes begin to well with tears, fogging
my view, as my nostrils are once again invaded
by the smell of oranges, desperately fighting
off the odor of gun powder and a couple
of silhouetted shapes in the grass, their arms
stretched out like those of the doll left behind.

THE BRIDGE

where was I really at that moment
when she said I should not let the past
pass me, for I'd be walking behind it
while believing I was getting away from it.

were those words, uttered unexpectedly,
almost as an afterthought, what made me
stop, still clutching my suitcase, or something
I thought I'd glimpsed in the dense coppice

as I watched her walk across the bridge,
two pear-shaped plastic bags in her hands
that held the whole future of her past
rocking in perfect harmony with her gait.

She stopped in the middle and glanced
back at me, the look on her face puzzled
and scared because I was not behind her:
Why aren't you coming? her body suddenly

awhirl in a grotesque pirouette, her hair
swaying like golden wheat in a gust
of wind, while I was trying to tell
myself that I had not heard anything,

and the only thing I was supposed to do
was to wheel about, drop my suitcase
like a dead weight, and start to run,
zig-zagging back toward my future

IN THE CLASSROOM

the night slowly chokes the light
around us   and she closes the book
her hand hovering above the cover
History Primer: A Short Guide

we look at each other
   as if trying to remember
each other's face before it becomes
   its own shadow

the building's roof's a charred skeleton
the classroom floor littered with textbooks
notebooks   the village half burned
deserted   except for one donkey

braying in the field   as the two of us
came down the road   two animals approaching
warily from the opposite direction
   trying to sniff each other out

she placed two hand-grenades
on the desk   that now look to me
like overgrown exotic pears
   we are going to feast on

History is supposed to teach us
something but it never does   she
almost yells   I look at the blackboard
   and make out its message

WE WILL BE BACK
a nauseous thought swells suddenly
in my stomach   I was here
before   she was here

before   closed the same book
when I said   It does not
because we never learn   anything
before or after
   she reached into her coat pocket
and I shot her   blindly
   to blot out all memory

You fainted   she explains
propping my head up   her face coming
and going together with a wavering candle

that makes the walls ebb away
and school desks flung in the corner
advance like ghosts toward us
            It's from hunger   I whisper

THE WAY THINGS HAPPEN

perhaps the only way for me
to retrieve my sanity is to accept
I imagined everything I believed
I had once remembered:

There was a house, in me, unfurnished,
but I was there, in that one-room
house, the only piece of furniture,
my rented life renewable every other year.

Then one day some people came,
the house was in their domain, they
declared, and had to be requisitioned,
leaving me an hour to pack and leave.

I got my gun and killed them all,
their children now, having tracked me
down in another land, demand I pay
them all uncollected property taxes.

They also included a dog-house I made
for a dog that had come to live with me,
until one morning I found his ears
and his tongue on my window sill.

That was when I realized I had
to disappear, and then they reappeared,
the same faces I had wanted to forget,
convinced I had done away with them.

So I got a gun I kept under floor
boards and shot myself, took off my ear,
and now I live in the park, and now I know
that everything happened exactly that way.

THE SUM OF EVERYTHING

**When you wake up tomorrow, everything
Will be forgotten,** mother used to say,
reaching for the lamp switch to consign
me to darkness beyond that of the eyes –

did that mean the next day neither she
nor I was going to know there was always
something we remembered we'd forgotten
to escape from oversleeping ourselves:

if we can at the very moment of death
remember everything, as in **My whole life
flashed before me:** then forgetting would
be complete, and everything, but we do not
know that, even if we die having uttered that:

a person who hears that cannot say **He
remembered everything, which allowed him
to forget it,** for nobody could claim this
possible, certainly not those who tried to
make the issue go away but now want me

to get up convinced we could start over,
as in **It's a new day and everything's just
fine,** which is what mother would say, throwing
the window panes wide open to have the light
blind me and turn in anger to the wall:

as I was made to do years later, waiting
for the bullet while staring at my own shadow,
trying to tell it not to fall together with me -

WALKING AWAY

there were perhaps a few things left
to be done,
           some crippled messages
that had to be carried
           before I returned to myself
           to see if something had been
left of me

    in the landscape of displaced memory,
where boundary marks are only disfigured
mounds, the mind begins to play hide-and-
seek with itself, trying to recover
what it was once forced to bury

    there was a house on the other side
of the field, and a figure standing before
it; he waited for the key that hung
on a chain around my neck, though the house
had its doors blown out,
                    which meant he
waited for me, to deliver myself, hoping
I'd escape with my life, my field of vision
to be kept as hostage

    the scene I come to now is different,
set by some other stage designers, yet I
see myself approach a figure with a key
that hangs on a chain around his neck,
my arms stretched out, fingertips ready
to feel his blank face,
                    when a bird
that rested for a moment on the barbed wire
takes wing, making me clench my fists
to hold the blood that oozes out of my palms
and walk away from myself

FRAMED MEMORIES

there came a day when everyone
was dodging sniper fire

a. a woman looking for godot and a tree,
   wearing a helmet and a flak jacket
b. a man conducting a crippled orchestra
   in the skeleton hall of muffled history
c. a woman getting short-stemmed flowers
   picked at impromptu cemeteries
d. a girl who sneaked out to find
   a market and a book of matches
e. a boy who ran among garbage mounds,
   trying to catch his strayed dog
f. an old blind woman who couldn't explain
   why she suddenly decided to leave the cellar

   d. e. and f. died that day
   - how do I know that?
   that day I died with them.

yet,
   d. keeps going out,
      although I got matches for her
   e. keeps searching, although I saw
      his dog float down the river
   f. keeps standing in the open, although I
      flail my invisible arms to make her go in

I watch them on my screen,
then turn off the colors
and gaze at the framed memories,
      waiting to see myself break out
      to give the girl her matches,
      find another dog for the lost boy,
      take the old blind woman by the hand
      and lead her down the street:

      the two of us smiling and feeling our way
      under a bright sun that casts no shadows

TRAVERSING

the mind stirs
        remembers itself
the body stays
        anchored in the echoless void
        from the axis down

muscle spasms
        that imitate the skeletal will
        power
weightless like the jagged piece of lead
        asleep in the cervical canal

the eyes
        that try to lure the sun
        into the window frame rotate it
around the column and have the locomotion
        rise in memory again

it is there that the gravity can be
        walked away from
    . prevented from conspiring
        with weight discharge
that mixes blood and urine

it is there where the point of departure
                is the point
of arrival
that the mind set in motion traverses
over the boundary of a receding horizon

THE AFTERMATH

there are some time-warped moments
when you manage to forget the war
although the war never forgets you:

it goes with you like your shadow, now
shorter, now longer, left of you, right
of you, now before you, now behind you:

it turns into you when the night
erases the horizon and makes
your mind become a blind navigator:

your reflexes are your compass as you
try again to find the way into space
where gravity doesn't force things

and memory to be in balance, your outline
to tell you, when you're up, whether you
left your legs in your sleep, or not

OF TIME, MEMORY, AND THE SOUL

1. have I come across my body lying supine
   on the sun-baked beach, a seagull trying
   to pick something out of my wide open mouth
   then looping off screeching when I raised
   my hand to chase it away, or defend myself:

2. to survive its own reasoning, memory
   is inclined to manipulate time, and time,
   on the other hand, always keeps on
   deconstructing the memory in order to
   avoid being reconstructed unsequentially:

3. having had no choice, I followed time
   to the end of measurable distances,
   all the while believing I was going
   back, hoping to find a salvation turn
   that may have been missed along the way:

4. perhaps I could claim I was not able
   to see a thing, asleep all the time,
   out with the soul, and going back was,
   in fact, moving on, for what was there,
   once, was not there any more

5. or: I could perhaps say I did not wake
   up at all and, thus, can not remember
   whether I had or had not awakened,
   whether, before or after that, I said
   I would be back on time, or in time

6. or: I ought to pretend that whatever
   portion of my life could be behind me
   may be retrieved if it's somewhere ahead
   of me, stored by the soul to have something
   to remember if one day it decides to return:

7. but I saw my body cast out on the sand,
   my mouth wide open, a seagull, about to pull
   something out, looped off screeching when I
   raised my hand, a senseless gesture, the soul
   long gone, indifferent to time and memory

HOMEWARD BOUND

I remember tomorrow, that was all
I said when I set out on the way home,
though, by the way, if there were a way by,
tomorrow must have already happened or I
would not have remembered it, which meant
even if I had arrived where I was supposed
to arrive, back home was there no more,
for I would've made it only to yesterday,
and wouldn't that have been the very day
when I said: I remember tomorrow –

still, I followed the rusty railroad tracks,
thinking they'd have to get me somewhere,
although they were overgrown with weed,
only here and there a meager looking flower
I hopped over or walked around, often losing
my step, until I came to a gate, a spider web
iron gate with a lock shaped like a heart
on a chain around someone's neck, but there
was neither a fence nor a wall at the right
or the left of it, except two track ruts going
on and fading into a breathing shimmering haze.

I stood there, to see whether another day,
the one before or the next, was on the other
side of the gate, but then a child appeared
as if he stepped through a curtain, jumping
unsteadily from one invisible sleeper onto
the other, from time to time flapping his arms
to maintain the balance, and he came to me,
his cheeks all puffed up, took a key
out of his mouth and unlocked the gate.

I could have gone around, I uttered, but he
smiled and said: Walls and fences are not absent
Because we do not see them, but you remembered
Tomorrow, so you can pass and go home with me.

he turned around and jumped onto the first patch
of scarred dirt, and I followed, the sleepers
getting farther apart, our leaps ever more daring,
and I waved my arms, and he flapped his, as if we
were going to leave the earth and fly up, still
two playful kids on their way home, not to be
caught out too late, overtaken by darkness.

END PHRASE

whatever was supposed to be
there was   not, so he
jumped on his horse
to ride off into the sunset
                          but the sunset
was not there either

                        so he turned
around his old iron maiden
and started to ride
                        into the sunrise
but a sign dropped
from the sky: due to phraseograph shortage
we are currently experiencing problems
with a new day   it read

which made him deduce that was a message
about something else
a horse of a different color
so he got off
and flipped a coin to see which way
to go   but the coin
remained hanging in the air

and that was the last straw   he took
his gun out
and pressed the barrel against his temple
realizing when he pulled the trigger
he must have run out of bullets

which meant he had probably killed
every single soul on the way
into this valley   yet he could not
remember   perhaps didn't even want to
though the gun was still warm
and he was in fact on the run
from the sound   he was somehow aware

of throughout

        causing now
        a piercing thought
to course through his head
there's no place for me to hide
        in this one-act play
        of fee-fie-foe

and the horse bolted away
        the moment
a snare drum burst
made him drop to his knees
his lips letting out hissing sounds:
    I just have to remember
    the watchword
    and this will be over
    for I will be awoken.

He turned his head and made out
a child sitting at a school desk,
scribbling something in his notebook.
There was suddenly snow in the air,
blinding his eyes, making his teeth chatter,
but he saw the child rip the page out
and bring it to him, lifting it up
with his transparent fingers, his eye sockets
two black buttons, the shiny pink face
that of a china puppet.

The sheet was white and blank.
    This is your table, the child
    said. And now you figure out
    Where you meet your end.

Two: Broken Lines
    (Notes
        toward a Quotidian Fiction)

THE QUESTION
OF THE BEGINNING AND THE END

many of them who were not
part of your story
wrote themselves in –
                    guest characters
                    they pretended to be,
waiting to see
          what you would do
          before they made their move

These are the pages I managed
To rescue, you said, some singed,
Smudged, covered with mortar dust,
Making it hard for me to recognize
My own handwriting, and unpaged,
So I can't say whether they are
Those of the beginning or the end.

you made an attempt to get out
- in the middle of the page –
          because you couldn't see any more
          what the end was going to be
- your end:
the act courageous or cowardly
- their end:
the act merciful or indifferent
          because you couldn't foresee
          if they had already designed it
- ultimately, perhaps,
because you forgot, or were forced
not to remember, how the story began

Which hand moved first,
The one that took the pen,
Or the one that took the sword,
you read,
          but there was no one

in the auditorium except a woman
that looked like someone's mother,
way up in the gallery, her eyes
closed, her mouth half-open

      - and then the lights went out

       you stopped and bowed,
a hand took you
by the hand,
escorting you behind the cyclorama,
a blank horizon suddenly lit,
showing troops marching towards you,
a child in your image leading them,
brandishing a wooden sword
to the beat of the soundless drum

A CONVERSATIONAL POEM
WITH A POST-MORTEM

you could not have gone
through all that and remained
alive, and of sound mind,
to write about, the voice says,
creating a hollow echo in my head,
for life, you know my dear, is
not a movie, let alone poetry:

I agree, my dear, and this
"my dear" is here for the rhythm's
sake, though we now have ample proof
that art often imitates life, do
we not, which blurs the difference
which way we want or have to go,
and, besides, you cannot really see
whether I'm alive just because you
may be at the moment of saying
this, and, by the way, mark the use
of the verb "may be," my dear:

are you trying to have me believe
you could've imagined everything
and made it look real enough
for you to survive it, or you did
so and had really gone through
to prove there was no difference
between the two, or, which would be
something bordering on insanity,
caused things to be just to show
what could've been imagined was, in
fact, what actually happened, thus
having made it prophetically un-real:

is that a question, and if it is
do you know whether or not the real I
will entertain a veritable answer,
and if you assume, whichever you do,

would you consider the possibility
I may be faking it, I mean the answer
that you, it seems, so eagerly await:

don't question my question, for I
see why you could be doing this, just
to prolong the whole matter because you
do not really know but need to put it
into a poem or some other convoluted
piece of writing to see which way
it really goes, and that may be why
you are so concerned with this thing
"rhythm," but isn't that because you
do not breathe, which may also be
why you touch every name at every plot,
as if to convince yourself yours is not
already there, burned into a wooden cross:

well, don't you realize that doing that
I myself try to figure out whether it
was the real I who survived the war,
or someone else that I now imagine
was me to deal with this in-saneness:

if it were the real you, sheer luck
got you through, sheer luck, you know
that my dear, and this repetition I
throw in for the sake of your rhythm,
but the gate is about to be closed
and I can easily fly over the fence,
something I'm sure you could not do.

*

I do not say anything though I know
I did that last night, jumped
over the wall on that lined sheet
of paper when the shrapnel in my head
moved closer to memory, but also did
that to prove I could, I could....

A POET ON THE SIDEWALK

a man dashed across the street
diagonally, his clenched fist aimed
at me, and collapsed before my feet.

everybody was looking at me as I
stood there, bending over the body,
though too stunned to do anything.

people started to gather, some
pointing at me, and I felt someone
from behind grab me in a bear hug.

with unfriendly faces around I
saw no point in resisting; I am
a poet, I muttered, a stranger here,

have never seen him. At this very
moment, I said aloud, I was thinking
about the next line in my poem.

but the voice behind breathed heavily
in my ear, the grip getting tighter: If
you weren't here, this wouldn't have

happened; this guy would not have died
the way he did, right at your feet,
which made me think I could have done

something to that man, in the past,
perhaps in that other land, and he
had recognized me and…, but what?

couldn't he be the enemy that once
had me fixed in his riflescope and
was now bent on finishing the job?

his face was contorted, revealing perhaps
the spasm of hatred, possibly astonishment
I was alive and thus could be a witness;

or, have I mentioned him in one of my poems
and he saw himself as a target, enraged
with what I had said or let be known?

....
my refugee papers having been checked,
promise given I would not try to leave
town if I were somehow needed again,

I walked out of the precinct two hours
later and went back to the same spot
on the sidewalk, hoping I might detect

something, his intent at the moment
of dying, yet all the time convinced the man
had something against my kind or poetry.

THE POWER OF POETRY

(**Back from the combat mission,** the reporter
said, **the pilots were tired, yet smiling,
some even quoting Shakespeare.**)

Eleven poets at the podium,
sitting on white plastic garden chairs
arranged in a row, and eleven
in the audience, scattered around
like apples a tree discards in autumn,
the former declaiming about war,
those down there applauding in unison:

at the next reading they change places,
the story does not change, the war
is still on, the poets, those sitting now
in the pit, applaud to their own refrains.

Then, while standing around the table
in the program director's crammed office,
twenty two poets eye light refreshments
and wait for someone to make a move
and open a single bottle of sparkling wine
that commands plastic cups formed in ranks,
all the while discussing the need
to make poetry reflect its fighting mission,
that of drawing people in and becoming
the driving force of their awareness:

when, in the end, a lone hand goes up,
holding high the empty cup, a hoarse voice
proclaiming, I'll drink to that if someone
can find a corkscrew and open the damn thing.

COMPATRIOTS AND ENEMIES

shuffling angrily down the supermarket aisle
one Saturday evening because I had to come
back and pick up something I had forgotten,
I almost slipped on a wet patch and slid
into an old skinny man with a mop and
a bucket that had suddenly materialized
before me. I mumbled a curse in my language
only to hear him echo it and sneer briefly.

my head jerked, gave a crick to the neck, and
our eyes met, a silent moment of recognition
followed by an eternity of nagging suspicion:
should I have approached him, asked him where
he was from, how he ended up there, working
in such a place, or simply taken him to be
a very good imitator, probably someone who had
no idea what the two words really meant –

the next time I came, my eyes surveying
the scene, I noticed him in the produce
section sorting strawberries, organic and,
what's that other word, unorganic/cultivated,
but he averted his eyes every time I looked
in his direction, trying to detect if his clothes,
features, gestures could tell me whether he was
one of those men who not long ago wanted me dead.

finally, one rainy afternoon I walked up
to him and said: I'm a poet, nothing for you
to worry about, the fatuous declaration
making me turn red. Me too, he whispered,
adding more loudly: I read your poetry long
ago; didn't particularly care about it. And
that was the last time we, the two compatriots
displaced from life, said anything to each other.

I got some ham and cheese, simply not to walk
out empty handed, all the while telling myself
he meant what he had said, and once I was
outside, swallowed by foggy night, I grinned,
relieved he was not that other kind of enemy.

AT THE WINDOW

how do you die in a land
that is not yours,
                    alien
to the dirt that has no memory
of your blood
         history

         what you were when you were
not
         what you are not when you can
be
    as long as you ration your sanity
    the way you did your food back there

slice by slice
         word by word
                  something by nothing

as you are asked to now, standing
at the window
on the eleventh floor,
                    thick glass
wedged in the metal and cement frame:
impenetrable,
              the height making you
dizzy, blurring the scene as you look
down
         at the square, trying to figure out
what those people that sit around the fountain
munch impassively during their lunch hour:

the water that swallows itself
enticing you to search for that blue expanse
beyond the buildings, the trees, flags,
and oblivion,
              where the air dances
above the mirroring calmness,
                  tempting you to go there,

a veil shrouded specter,
and swim away,
                    free at last
from the gravitational weight of the mind

                    that keeps pulling you
down where mother sits, eating voraciously,
picking crumbs like a pigeon between her legs,
murmuring, while food spatters from her mouth:

        Even if we survive all this, my son,
        We shall never be alive again,
        So it doesn't matter how,
                            or where we die.

RESTORATION

colorless pigments dance before the eyes
creating homeless pictures in the mind

the lining tissue is permanently scarred
the brain a hostage to the fibrillating past

how much time does the memory have left
when counting goes from one hundred back

a blade draws the line and the flesh
responds like a flower in the morning sun

the light never manages to recognize its shadow
nor the smooth vessel muscles their skeletal brothers

when the mouth gag is removed the tongue
remembers nothing except its own weight

*

it is too early to say what the outcome
will be though more will be known later on

once the motor functions are restored
as well as the will to forget and come back

MISE EN SCENE

I heard a seagull screech, pursuing
relentlessly another with a piece
of bread in its mute yellow beak
        :was it just food or an excuse
to do harm –
        two indistinguishable ballet
dancers on the stage, pirouetting
against the painted azure sky,
power lines, and scabby oak trees,
        or two planes, looping up
and down, not after the food any more
but the ultimate prize: life itself –

could I have known which one
saw that piece first,
                        which one
wanted it more because of hunger
or sheer desire to subjugate the other,
claim victory over that patch of land –

I went and threw the dumpster
flaps open, rotting food in plastic bags
penetrating my nostrils,
                        the smelling salts
my neighbor shoved under my nose
when I fainted from hunger one summer
day in the suffocating cellar –

        Here, here, you idiots, I yelled,
        Come on, you ugly bastards, here –

my words the exact ludicrous replica
of those I had shouted staggering
                        across the empty square,
shrapnel holes resembling some deliberate
                        ornamental design,
my eyes, a madman's, trying to detect
sharpshooters behind the trees

         on the sizzling hillside,
  trees like those
now hiding the two warring seagulls –

and while I stood there, feeling
the saliva slowly foam in the corners
of my mouth,
        one returned,
out of nowhere, swooping toward me,
           dropping on the cement
a brownish-white bomb that splattered
like a piece of a brain,
       when a sudden wind draft
made it climb to the sky,
together with the remnants of that slice,

       leaving me to wonder
helplessly whether the returnee was
      the one that had salvaged it,
      or had it as a war booty –

An hour later I came out again and found
A man throwing an old tv and two
Huge garbage bags into the dumpster,
Murmuring: Some people have no manners,
Never learned to close the fucking thing.

FOOLS OF FATE

during the war our two rooms
were requisitioned
      by some austrian soldiers /
they came one showery day
and for two weeks mother and I
slept at night in the basement
      / poor young men,
she would say, conscripted,
      do not really want to fight,
      just go home to their cows,
      meadows, and pigs /

they gave me a sausage, a slice
of dark bread, and candy I
almost choked on, the sergeant
having to turn me upside down
      as if to hang me by my feet / I
      cried because I spat it out
    / that I do not remember,
but I do the stench / from time
to time
      it worms itself
      into my nostrils,
      their rain and sweat soaked army coats
      smelling of rotten leaves, their feet,
      big toes protruding out of their socks,
      reeking of pungent sauerkraut /

life already decomposing
      / leaving them nothing to take
back home / most not even themselves /

or /   is that my odor,
    all along
    reminding me repeatedly
  what my fate is
  / no point in yelling: Not the same
  thing /   if things are

the same,
the design allows minor variables /

So,
I went to a small austrian town
  mother used to talk about long after
  the morning we found them gone,
  a piece of paper with the address
  pinned to the door,
tracked down a distant relative of the sergeant,
    an old blind woman
    who claimed I was one of them,
    back at last:
  Du bist zurickgekommen.
  Wo warst du? she squeaked

what was the point of my coming,
  to convince myself my odor
  from another war was not the same,
and she let me know that was immaterial,
  as if it were not, always /

  I was lost but have found my way
back,
  I whispered to her /
      and left

IN THE SUPERMARKET HALF A WORLD AWAY

I pick up a glossy tomato and
squeeze it, unspoken words bleed
through my fingers, the skin
splits along imaginary seams,

I am a regular customer so
the supermarket manager looks
at me without saying anything:
This is how my mind bleeds,

I mumble and move on, pushing
the cart, knowing he follows
at a polite distance, stops when
I place my hand on crushed ice

between fish trays, focusing on
the eye of a trout that reflects
me, then puncture the plastic,
gouge the eye and swallow it,

feeling the manager's disgusted
look on my back, his spasm gripped
mouth, when I turn, that of the trout,
half open, just like mine after I

was netted, the trout's head, I now
recall, a man's charred blue face
with one nacreous socket I caught
for a brief moment on television

the night before, amid strewn fruit,
pomegranates, red oranges, tomatoes,
blown-up meat and flesh, and I start
to push, stumbling after the stretcher's

crooked wheels, toward the crimson lettered
sign: Express Lane Ten Items Or Fewer,
tears of pained anger welling in my eyes,
the trout bouncing at the grate-like bottom
as if to persuade me it is still alive
and I saw only what I could not have seen

SOONER OR LATER

Mountain peaks jutting up
Like broken teeth, rounded tops
Swollen like bellies about to go
Into labor, together with everything
Down here, are merely the sky's bottom,
he whispered, swaying in front of me
like some bird losing its bearings,
And the air is nothing else but
A dried-up ocean in which they
Still fish us with dynamite.
Sooner or later you'll see what I
See if you hear my whole story.

I glanced at an orange plastic water
pistol tucked in his waist and waved
him off, my hand remaining in the air
as if waiting for the other to surrender
as well, but he continued to sway
by the table, his right hand empty
jacket sleeve pinned to the pocket
into which I had thoughtlessly stuffed
enough money for a drink or two.

You'll be allowed to rise to the surface
Sooner rather than later, he proclaimed,
having taken the money out with his left hand,
and moved slowly two tables away from mine,
making three young men burst into laughter,
their thumbs pointing up, left and right
index finger pulling a trigger mockingly.

I sat staring numbly at the open window
in the building across the street,
my memory suddenly invaded once again
by the sound blasting from a tape
recorder in the room's yawning darkness:
Sooner or later I'll get you, you
Know; I'll be patient and so will you,

For you have nothing else to do
But wait for me to come to you.
The lyrics of the old love song used
not so long ago to make people come
out of the dark cellar, with one hand
up, the other clutching whatever was
left of their forgotten life.

I looked around, but the man was gone,
and so were the three young men,
the waitress appearing at my side:
Sir, we are about to close now.

Sooner or later you'll have to, sooner
Rather than later, I muttered, oblivious
to her puzzled look, and went in search
of an open café and the man with one
hand and the plastic water pistol,
my aluminum leg adjusting slowly
to the rhythm of the other as I quickened
my pace, gulping the sultry night air.

EXECUTION

on a clear sunny day   a raincoat
draped over your clasped hands,
                hanging limp
in front of you   like a sail
on a windless sea,
hides the handcuffs

                almost
a leisured walk
from a chartered jet to a car
with tinted windows

once there
            a quick turn, a glance
searching for the camera,
                invisible
                on the spectators' terrace:
no smile, no sign of recognition,

for who remembers whom
as I touch the screen,
                    my forefinger
electrified, resting for a moment
on your genocidal forehead,
                    the mind
squeezing a trigger
                the avenging finger
penetrating your skull:
you are   gone –

I hop back to my chair,
                    the crutches,
one on each side, upright,
like two masts I stared at, waiting,
one rainy day   in Rotter
dam
and look back at my hand
            still stuck to the screen

where now on an endless sandy beach,
somewhere   in the Baha
mas
a young woman with flowing golden hair
rides a beautiful black stallion,
foamy waves racing to his hoofs are sucked
back in
          dragging with them my hand,

          and a sign
          pasted on the fathomless sky
offers me a vacation of a lifetime

OF BELONGING

a man
> in the middle
> of the road
> his white shirt drenched by rain
> the pants splashed by swerving cars

waves his arms in slow motion
as if trying to downshift
even arrest all motion

I pull onto the shoulder
and get out
focusing on something
at his feet
> my mind cluttered
> with images that should have been
> removed long ago:

> a contorted body hit by a sniper
> a dog shot for fun –

there's no house around
and I do not see his car
yet I run across
ducking my head instinctively
and make out a dog
one eye open as though waiting
for the command
to stop playing dead

D'you need help –
> my words are drowned by a siren
> our presence dwarfed
> by two descending silhouettes

> Get back in your car – one yells

I do not move
> Get off the road Now – the other bellows

the man doesn't move

I am grabbed and I resist
the man is grabbed and he resists

> The cold black leather
> of the patrol car's back seat
> smells the same as the one I
> was on, one eye gazing at a void
> like that dog's, my palm pressed
> against the ribs to block
> the bleeding from a shrapnel wound.

> was I dragged from the pavement –
> or did I drag someone from the pavement –
> whose drops of blood spattered
> on the cement like a lazy summer shower –

The raindrops at the headlights become
white fluttering moths, and the man
from the open road, sitting next to me,
turns his head and smiles:

Is that your dog – I hear myself ask
Isn't that now your dog too – I hear him say

A NOTE. A DOT.

if to survive, he wrote, didn't imply
to live beyond but to continue to exist
only Figuratively, According to the prefix,
I was left with Nothing divided by Nothing,
yet made to accept I still got something.

He came out of the cellar and started
to walk, creating an ever greater distance
between his mind and his body, or
the other way round, neither smiling
nor crying, or maybe a little bit of both.

to Outlive death one has to live it out,
the note went on, pinned askew to the back
of his winter coat hung grotesquely
on a rusty hook, but to Outlive life –
four dots following threw everything off.

I could've tried to stop him, at least
shout if afraid to run out, for I saw
the rope in his hand, yet desperately hoped
the trees in the park a block away must
have been blown up or cut down for fire

wood, so only my eyes followed him,
my twisted neck having my cheek glued
to the frosted window, until he became
a meandering dot among the ruins covered
almost mercifully by soothing whiteness.

THE QUESTION OF SIDES

time was not on his side, and
life, come to think of it, was not
on his side either, left or right:

on one side a field he would've needed
three minutes to run across and reach
the river that, swelling, promised nothing,
on the other, a church with a machine
gun nest in the belfry window, keeping
time for those whose time had expired.

which side are you on, a neighbor crouching
on the staircase one night demanded
to know, and he said: on your side
at my side if we faced in the same direction:

the bell rope tied, still the tongue chattering
blindly behind him as time was measured
by twigs snapping under his feet, his eyes
already on the other side, the body plunging in,
letting the lungs exhale crimson bubbles.

: on the other bank downstream, gaffed
and pulled into the shallows two days later,
he was looked at briefly: the calm face no one
could've remembered: then pushed off, his arms
spread out as if trying to span the shores
while he gently sailed on before the wind:

WHAT I WANT TO SAY

if it were plausible to gauge
the top and the bottom leveling
limit and thus escape death
in between, I would not be
alone now, without my wife
who could not see that, and
my dog who couldn't see that,
stranded on this vast island
that looks like unconquered land,
yet swarms with forlorn souls
that search for a veritable answer
to the question: what am I
looking for here if the leveling
of limitless opportunities is
to pin-point the limits of
opportunity, and though I keep
telling myself: I am looking
for a wife, my wife, and I am
looking for a dog, my dog,
the war is still on, and it
is not my war, yet it seems
I am not able to get out of wars,
a remnant of the old slogan:
we shall live as if peace will
last for ever and a war break
out tomorrow, its logic implying
reciprocal causality and thus
mutual exclusion, which is not
that far from what we resort to
these days: we can talk, but we
have really nothing to say
to each other, so the only thing
we shall end up with is to agree
to disagree, and that often leads
to this: both sides may be right,
and wrong, so we'll have a truce
and then let each side play on
according to its own conception

of reality, which is certainly
what a child in the park entertains,
coming to me in the fenced-off
area, saying: my dad is not around,
and I refrain from gauging the sense
of his words, so you can now play
with me, you'll be a skeleton and
I'll be a pirate because I have
the sword, swishing before my eyes
with a blade, a battery-powered
fluorescent blue rod which I know
belongs to another movie, so I ask,
pointing at the plastic structure
with turrets, walkways, and chambers
whose windows have been blown out:
can that be my space ship, and
the child yells: you play my game
and in my game you get killed
at the end, so I look at his mother
as if pleading for her help
to sort out, if nothing else,
chimeric realities, but she does
not move, keeps standing outside
the theater, staring at me as if I
were an enemy unworthy of being
played with and done in, her german
shepherd on the leash, immobile,
ears up, waiting for a command
that had my uncle, whose name I
inherited, pass water in his pants
at the transport train platform,
though I was almost at the point
of asking her whether, once playing
is finally done, she could be
my wife, even her dog my dog,
but now I suddenly turn away,
realizing I am right in the middle
between the two of them, so I run
out of the playground, away from
the swings, slides, and sand boxes
with unexploded mines, and keep

on running, again, telling myself
this time I could, I have to, get
to the end, of the island, the earth
itself, simply step off, drop
into the airless silence to take
a deep breath and shout at the top
of my voice: I was there, I played
all the games, and what I want to say
is:

SLIDES

pictures that keep coming
as if someone forgot to shut off
a slide projector and you do not know
where the power box is in your head:
    a man whose entrails are scooped
    back in as though a duffel bag
    got ripped open and things plopped out
you strain your ears to hear a warning
some images may be too graphic
justifying your going into the kitchen
to take something and avoid yourself
yet you stay needing proof it won't be
you in one of those dead frames:
    there every body covered by a sheet
    can be you every charred head have
    your bone structure and the same number
    of horse-like front teeth sticking out:
    an arm picked up like a piece of wood
    and placed on a cart makes you cross
    your arms to feel they're still there,

and so on and so on without end,
he said, sitting in the bleached room
with one painted window her figure split
down the middle, leaving one side
for the lunar, one, for the solar eye.

    Do you dream in color,
    she asked,
looking out at the tree crown exploding
in green, which he saw only as leaves
framing her shingled head, its midnight
black shade having him make out a tank
muzzle camouflaged by branches.

In Technicolor, he said, his face a grimace.

We could give you something
To ease or eliminate color intensity.

Really? he blinked. How about the pictures?

Those we cannot do anything about.
We are not that powerful or charitable.

THE COLOR OF BLOOD

Whenever the sunset horizon was flushed
with the color of blood, mother would
cross herself and say under her breath:
God help us, there's going to be a war.

That late afternoon when I first laid
My eyes on you, she mused aloud one night
while I held a receiver in my hand, watching
the lightning set the sky ablaze, Two streaks
Of blood were on your cheeks, your screaming
Was like a battle-cry, and for a moment I
Resented the sight of you because of the pain
You caused me coming into this world, but I
Knew you'd not grow up to be a war dog.

While I was wheeled on a clanking stretcher
that wobbled down the corridor, fighting
the blood that oozed down my throat, I caught
a glimpse of a woman on the examination table,
holding her belly like leavened bread dough,
her hands the color of her red blouse, the nurse's
trying frantically to move them and scissor
the soaked fabric: Where's the entry wound,
and the doctor's rasping voice: The baby first,
trailing behind me as a double door burst
open for the lifeless light to receive me.

On the horizon, ten years later, another night
of exile seeps down the sky's crimson glow
as I stand at the window and watch the sun
get swallowed by the open sea, my fingers
tracing the scar's ridge along the lower jaw
to make sure the shrapnel is no longer there,
the pain now only in my memory, so I can go
to bed, close my eyes, and have the color
of blood fade for a while from consciousness.

RELATIONS

The unearthly clatter takes me once again
To the window to look at the cars
Of a freight train that drags itself
Like a well-fed anaconda: The Sierras,
Southern Service, Wisconsin, Detroit.

With a package of soft rye bread in one hand
And 12oz. pre-sliced cheese in the other,
I watch, my mind ready to embark on a journey
Whose purpose lies beyond its own destination,
Just as my grandmother's brother had done,
Staring perhaps at the same unending train,

His bundle a sweater with moth holes,
A shirt of unrecognizable color, a tin cup
Tucked inside, the whole thing belted,
Under his smelly armpit, as he was trying
To spot an unlatched door to clamber on
And go west, find some work to buy a ticket
And sail to what in his mind would
At the end have become east again.

He had jumped ship to make money
On dry land, he wrote his younger sister
In Fiume, the only postcard ever received,
With a grainy picture of a huge lady
I would gaze at silently as a child,
Her torch of stone flames high up in the air,
Some spiky crown on her head, and his PS
Scribbled on the white strip at the bottom:
I think I chose the wrong time to jump.

Found in a switch yard at dawn one day
When temperature turned the lake's lips
Into bluish frozen cotton candy,
Feverish, half-naked, with his belt
Around his neck, he yelled to the guard
Weigh Anchor, Weigh Anchor, and was gone.

I pour steamy coffee into my earthen mug,
When my late mother's words come to me:
Everyone in our family is fated to perish
In some foreign parts, whether he wants that
Or not, and I break into a stupid chant:
Weigh anchor, O, my past and future ghosts,
Here's to you and me, Weigh anchor again,
Weigh anchor, O, my known, my unknown ghosts.

THE ORDER OF THINGS

if I could explain
        to the dead   how
I stayed alive
when   why
I died   went unexplained to the living

        if in the displaced memory
I stopped   nowhere at somewhere
in a dead-end land   looking at the bones
dressed in rotting clothes   of those
who ended   somewhere at nowhere

did I recognize myself
that december day of my birth
        in someone else's coat
        as I went around the pit
gulping back the starved air

did I come to realize
in the village warehouse
     with its cement floor hosed down
     its walls streaked with faded blood
that I'd survived for I didn't know better

driven by hunger   or a wanton urge
to kill   when I trapped a pigeon
under a cardboard box   my bait
a dead earthworm in its beak   all of us
just extras in the natural order of things

if that was why   I set the pigeon free
and went back to the edge of the pit
to sit with the dead   why I ate
pieces of clay   to become
what I must have been   earth

THE OTHER SIDE

You'll get through this, she said.
I was looking at the wall, trying
to figure out what could be behind it –
another wall, a city, an open space,
another woman who would also tell me,
having caught me staring at the wall,
that I would be able to go through.
I don't mean the wall, she said,
her face straining to keep a calm look.
This situation, well, not this, really.
Oh, you know what I mean, don't you?

I didn't. I mean, I did not know.
Or maybe I did. Should have known.

The sun prickled my skin, but I managed
to discern my image in the wall, as if
it appeared slowly in a blurred mirror.
A small bird descended, its wings still
for a moment, and pecked at something.
A tremendous pain shot through my eye.
Blood started to course down the wall
as though someone wanted to restore
the primary color to the old faded bricks.
The bird hopped a few yards to the left
and I lost vision in my right eye.

Stumbling forward I finally touched
My grainy face, realizing all of a sudden
I was through, feeling the windless air.
You are a real illusionist, I heard her
shout behind me. What do you see there?

OF BREATHING AND LIVING

if I were able, even for a moment, to know
whether my soul is praying for me
when I can no longer hear my breathing –

with a frozen picture in the eyes whose surface
has been cracked by the light
that compressed oxygen into one mute dot,

globular words drying on the lips
that slowly take the color of dirt,
some though still left in the mind's alley,

hoping against hope they will at the end
find their way out, whole, and
not as syllables that had to be amputated,

making whoever is around look to the heavens
and turn away, unfulfilled, left
for ever with nothing but a vague conjecture

what the final message might have been, either
to or from, perhaps a variant later to be
used when memory takes a calculated detour –

I would feel, despite all that, the soul left
me dream on and I was brought about the next day
ignorant of the breath that was wasted on living

THERE AND HERE

if there are days, years when the mind
turns itself off, wanders out of time,
in order to survive, one's only hope
is that it will be somehow called back.

maybe that's why i sleep with the light
on and from time to time tie my mind
to a bedpost, or put it under the pillow,
my hand resting on it all night long.

however, i don't have a phone; whenever
i picked it up, a voice would say: Sorry
Wrong number, though i knew it wanted
to check whether i was still there.

and i don't answer my mail; in fact, there
isn't any mail to answer now, unless i
wish to pick a cemetery plot; displaced
from home, i'm already marked: prospect.

You think too much, mother would say,
And that is poisoning your mind, so i look
unabsorbed here; i put all theres and thens
in boxes and buried them at different places.

but, i do act as though i am not, as people
say, all there, and sometimes i am truly not,
especially when i believe my mind has gone
to find a then of now and a here of there.

it presumes hindsight madness, if exposed,
should foreshadow foresight sanity, but i think
it tries to see whether someone who's run
out of life could still be all there and here.

FIRST DAY OF SPRING

there were those who watched us
hide in frozen open graves, the dead
in the coffins above, their blood already
crystallized mud, holding their breath
not to be found out and killed again

and there were those who pretended
they saw and knew nothing, who talked
themselves out of truth in order to live
an abridged version of history,
cleansed of all the guilt of memory

and there were those, and I was one,
who thought the dead would in the end
lift the weight of the past so we could
know why we ran into the future
when life had been taken away from us

*

there are now those who tell me: you
got a country, at least on a piece
of paper that's nice, almost parchment-like,
waterproof and grease resistant, no doubt
treated with sulfuric acid, though the photo

is awful, like a mug shot, dull-eyed look,
hollow cheeks, sagging lower lip, you either
suffer from something, probably indigestion,
or torture yourself for no reason, only
because you expected too much from the dead

*

there it is, folks, I heard the weather man
say last night, first day of spring tomorrow,
and it's going to be a delicious sunny day
with feathery clouds sailing across the sky

your children can make into swans and Caspars.

there is a plot of land across from the cemetery,
once a park, now fenced off to be turned into
a subsidized apartment complex, a man made pond,
soon to be drained, still there with a stone swan
anchored in the middle of the inverted sky, as if
waiting for me to cross over, which I'll do, the two
of us to fly off weightless into the blue yonder

TELLING STORIES

where do I go from here if where I
came from turned out to be nowhere

and how do I tell you that now
when unscripted deeds lord over words:

for the sake of bare survival I traded
instincts for second-hand reflexes

but there are only so many ways to breathe
and read the trajectory of the past

what to hold off and what to hold on
as zero degree defines the angles:

could that have been the reason
I left you in another story: to save you

or to save myself and come to this
point wrapped in your frayed army

coat stained with blood I don't
remember whether yours or mine

as if to see how much space there is
left before we run out of time

before the stories run out of words
and we end up with nothing to tell

having been devised by someone else
who may have already rewritten the future.

ABOUT THE AUTHOR

Mario Susko, a witness and survivor of the war in Bosnia, moved to the US in 1993, where he received his M.A. and Ph.D. from SUNY Stony Brook in the early 70s. He has lived in the US two-thirds of the past 40 years, and currently teaches in the English Department at Nassau Com. College in Garden City, NY. Mario Susko is the recipient of several awards, including the 1997 and 2006 Nassau Review Poetry Award, the 1998 Premio Internazionale di Poesia e Letteratura *Nuove Lettere* (Naples, Italy), the 2000 Tin Ujevic Award for *Versus Exsul* for the best book of poems published in Croatia in 1999, the 2003 SUNY Chancellor's Award for the Excellence in Scholarship and Creative Activities, and the 2008 Editor's Choice Award in Poetry given by *Relief: A Quarterly Christian Expression*. His poem "Conversion," published and nominated by *Dream Catcher* (UK) was short-listed for the 2004 Forward Poetry Prize. The author of 28 poetry collections, Susko is also known as an editor and a translator of novels by Saul Bellow, William Styron, Bernard Malamud, E. L. Doctorow, James Baldwin, Donald Barthelme, and poetry by Theodore Roethke, e. e. cummings, among others, as well as the integral edition/translation of Walt Whitman's *Leaves of Grass*. His recent books include an anthology of Jewish-American short stories "A Declaration of Being," which he co-edited with Myron Schwartzman and translated into Croatian, and poetry collections *Eternity on Hold* (Turtle Point Press, 2005), the Croatian edition of the book (Meandarmedia, 2006), *Life Revisited: New and Selected Poems* (Allahabad, India, 2006), *Closing Time* (Harbor Mountain Press, 2008), the Croatian Edition (Meandarmedia, 2009), as well as a chapbook *Rules of Engagement* (erbacce-press, Liverpool, UK, 2009). His poems have been published in journals and anthologies in the US, UK, Croatia, Italy, Russia, Hungary, Ireland, India, Sweden, and Austria, among others.